Doggie Tales

Written & Illustrated
by
Phyllis Forbes Kerr

Published by
Walrus Productions
Seattle

Copyright 1998 by Phyllis Forbes Kerr

All rights reserved. Written permission must be secured from the publisher to use or reproduce any part of this book, except for brief quotations in critical reviews or articles.

Published by Walrus Productions
4805 NE 106th St. Seattle, WA 98125   (206) 364-4365

web site www.aa.net/walrus
e-mail walrus@aa.net

Written & Illustrated by Phyllis Forbes Kerr
Layout and typography by Larry Wall @ The Durland Group
Edited by Teri Gillet
Printed by Vaughan Printing, Nashville, Tennessee

Library of Congress Catalog Card Number 98-60803

Kerr, Phyllis Forbes.
   Doggie Tales / Phyllis Forbes Kerr

   ISBN 0-9635176-9-4
  1. Dogs--Humor. 2.Dogs--Humor, Pictorial. I. Title

Printed in the United States of America

10 9 8 7 6 5 4 3 2 1

Dedicated to:

My cousin Ellie who loves dogs
In memory of Mirra and Pancho
and my Dusty

Doggie Tales

How do dogs greet you when you come home?

Doggie Tales

With a Welcome Waggin'

Doggie Tales

How do dogs say hello in France?

Doggie Tales

Bonejaw

What do you call
a pup who gets
its second set of teeth?

Doggie Tales

Newfangled

9

How do dogs lose their fur?

Doggie Tales

On Shedule

Doggie Tales

When dogs want to eat fish, they like to...

Doggie Tales

Howl-a-bit

Doggie Tales

A dog who is bossy
with her pups is...

Doggie Tales

What do dogs like for breakfast?

Doggie Tales

Why do dogs
like new leads?

Doggie Tales

They get a new leash on life

Doggie Tales

How do dogs stay up on what's new?

Doggie Tales

What do people say when their dogs run away?

Doggie Tales

Dog Gone!

23

Why do senior dogs like visiting Yellow Bone National Park?

They're old faithfuls

Doggie Tales

How does
a dog race begin?

Doggie Tales

How do dogs describe what they roll in?

Doggie Tales

Heaven Scent

29

Doggie Tales

What do you call a dog who only cares about treats?

Doggie Tales

A biscuit case

Doggie Tales

What do dogs commonly fight over?

Bones of contention

Doggie Tales

What expression is used when a dog performs perfectly at a show?

Doggie Tales

Everything went off without an itch

Doggie Tales

A dog who has lots of puppies is called...

Doggie Tales

A Litter-Bug

How do you describe a dog who retrieves a ball?

Doggie Tales

Very fetching

What kind of book
is a favorite with dogs?

Doggie Tales

Scratch and Sniff

Doggie Tales

Describe a dog
who itches too much...

Doggie Tales

He's fleaworthy

Doggie Tales

What is a hound's most popular paw wear?

Doggie Tales

Rebarks

What dance do dogs like best?

Doggie Tales

The Fango!

47

Doggie Tales

When a dog
gets lots of bones, it's ...

Doggie Tales

A boneanza

How do dogs
get your attention?

Doggie Tales

They hound you

Doggie Tales

What do you call a dog who sniffs too much?

Doggie Tales

Too scentimental

What do dogs like best in *Playdog* magazine?

Doggie Tales

The scenter fold

Doggie Tales

A dog's favorite music

Bark & Roll

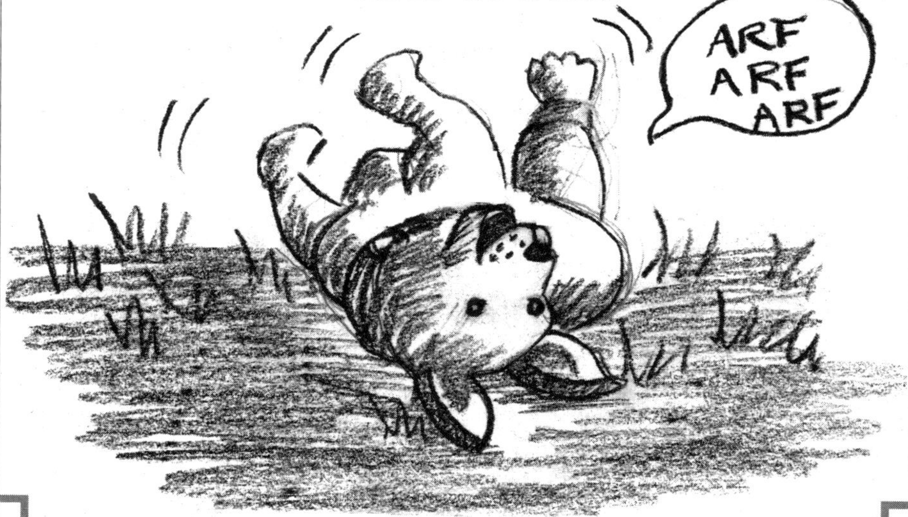

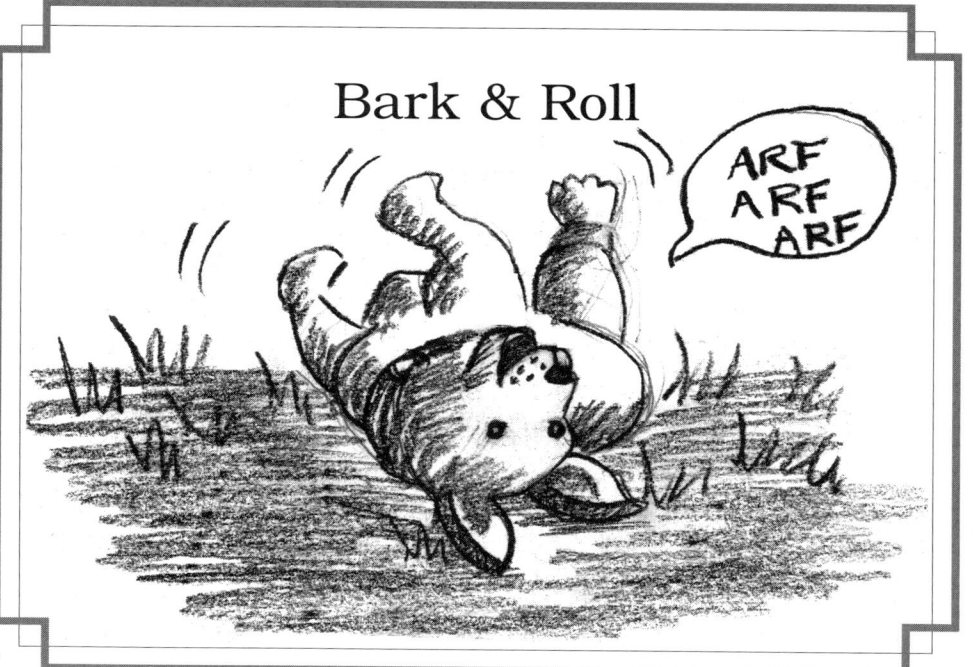

Doggie Tales

A dog who waits
at the front door is…?

Doggie Tales

a door mutt

What do you fear
when your dog runs away?

Doggie Tales

He'll do something trash

Doggie Tales

What do dogs dislike at the beach?

Doggie Tales

sanditches

Doggie Tales

What do dogs dislike after playing in the mud?

groom service

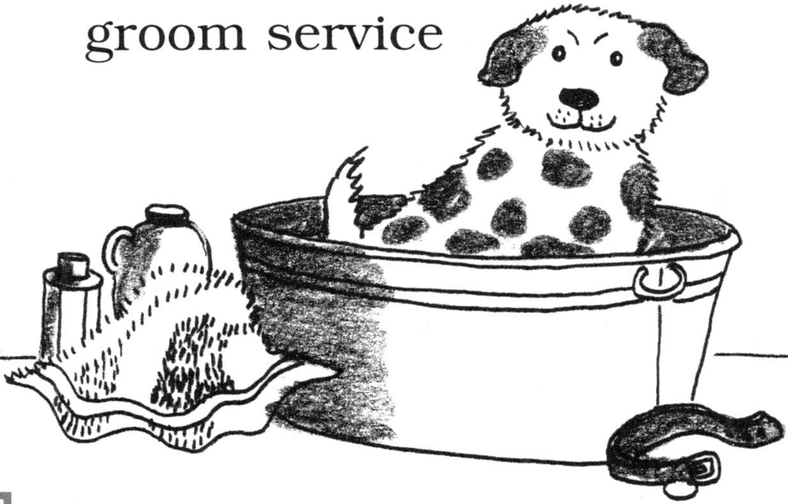

What board game do dogs like playing?

Doggie Tales

Barkgammon

Doggie Tales

A dog who O.D.'s on treats is...

Doggie Tales

Boned

What do dogs like best about baseball?

When the Ump yells, "Play Ball"

Dogs who like to *put on the gloves*

Doggie Tales

Boxers

The most religious dog

Doggie Tales

A Golden Believer

What kind of art work do dogs prefer?

Doggie Tales

prints

A famous illustrator who portrayed American life

Doggie Tales

Norman Barkwell

Dog Art:
A famous master piece

Doggie Tales

Bona Lisa

Describe a teething puppy

Doggie Tales

Very chewsy

Doggie Tales

What was the signal of revolutionary dogs?

Doggie Tales

One sniff by land, two sniff by sea

A famous dog food preparation contest

Doggie Tales

Bark Off with Betty Cocker

Doggie Tales

What do you call 13 dogs?

Doggie Tales

A Barker's Dozen

Doggie Tales

How do dogs avoid paying rent?

Doggie Tales

They break their leashes

How does puppy kindergarden begin?

Doggie Tales

with a Roll Call

What card game do dogs like least?

Doggie Tales

Old Spayed

What common ailment do dogs suffer from?

Doggie Tales

Highpawtension

Dogs who like
to ride in the car are...

Doggie Tales

bark seat drivers

Doggie Tales

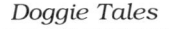

When a car has more
than one dog in it...

Doggie Tales

it's a car drool

Doggie Tales

If the U.S. used a dog
as its national symbol,
it would be…

Doggie Tales

The American Bald Beagle

Who is the patron saint of dogs?

Doggie Tales

Bone of Bark

Doggie Tales

What song do dogs sing at Christmas?

Doggie Tales

"Bark the Herald Angels Sing"

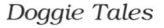

What degree do pups
get from obedience school?

Doggie Tales

Barkalaureates

Doggie Tales

How do dogs describe something close by?

Doggie Tales

It's a bone's throw away

Two famous American Frontier Dogs

Doggie Tales

Daniel Bone & Davy Barkit

Doggie Tales

What dog (named Duke) starred in the movie "Chew Grit?"

Doggie Tales

John Dane

A famous dog musical...

Doggie Tales

"The Hound of Music"

Doggie Tales

What dog had the lead role
in a movie called
The Collar Purple?

Doggie Tales

Wolfy Goldberg

Doggie Tales

A romance movie starring Richard Grrrr

Doggie Tales

Kitty Woman

A novel written by William Faulkner

Doggie Tales

The Hound & the Furry

The host of a game show called
"You Bit Your Wife"

Doggie Tales

A famous workout dog

Doggie Tales

Itchard Simmons

127

Doggie Tales

A powerful French emperor

Doggie Tales

Nipoleon Boneapart

Doggie Tales

What songs did medievel religious dogs sing?

Doggie Tales

Gregorian Pants

Doggie Tales

Regarded as one
of the greatest composers
of all time

Doggie Tales

Johann Sebastian Bark

Doggie Tales

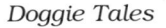

What ballet do dogs like best?

Doggie Tales

"The Muttcracker Sweet"

The star of Scent of a Woman?

Doggie Tales

Howl Poochino

Movie based on a novel
by Pant Conroy

Doggie Tales

"Prints of Tides"

Doggie Tales

A novel by Bark Twain

"The Prints and the Pawpurr"

Vietnam War Movie

Doggie Tales

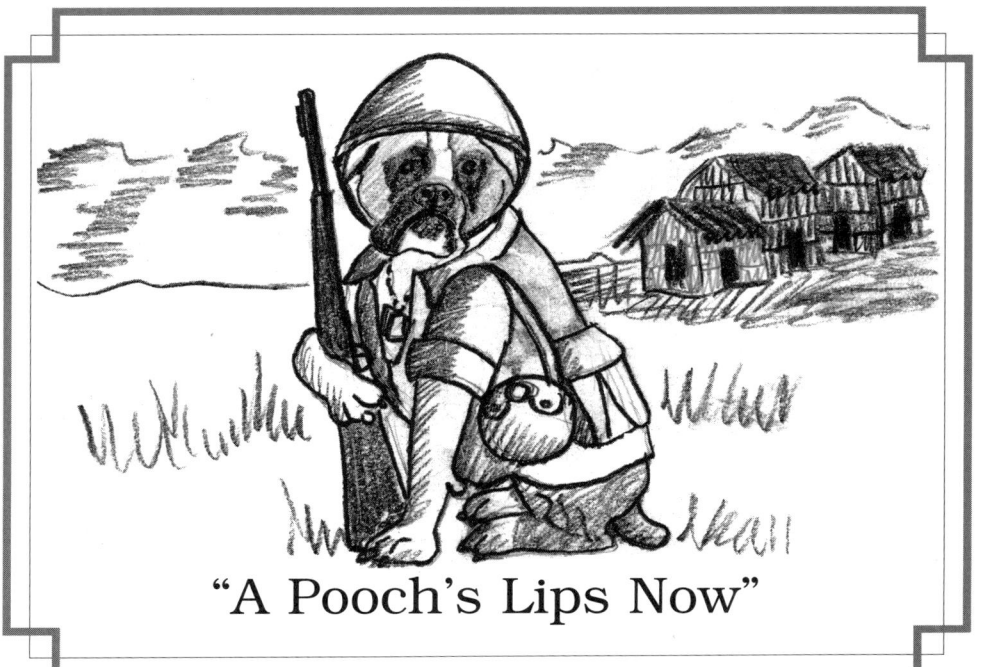

"A Pooch's Lips Now"

The most confident dog

Doggie Tales

The Cocky Spaniel

The most feminist dog

Doggie Tales

The Doberperson

Doggie Tales

The smartest dog is...

Doggie Tales

The Sharpie

If dogs could fly what would they say?

Doggie Tales

How you feel at the end
of a long, long day

Doggie Tales

dog tired

Doggie Tales

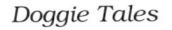

How does a dog get on a cruise ship?

Doggie Tales

He embarks

Doggie Tales

How do dogs say good bye in Italian?

Doggie Tales

ABOUT THE AUTHOR

Phyllis Forbes Kerr lives in Cambridge, Massachusetts with her husband Andrew, her golden retriever, Clover and tiger cat, Sparkey. She is a Wheelock graduate & former kindergarten & first-grade teacher who holds a masters degree from Lesley College as a reading specialist.

She is the author & illustrator of "Kitty Litterature" a humorous cat book, several children's books and most recently compiled & edited <u>Letters from China</u> (1838-1840 Canton-Boston correspondence of her great-great-grandfather, Captain Robert Bennet Forbes).

Phyllis has a successful line of greeting cards under the name JoyPhyl Greetings.

OTHER FUN BOOKS

A whimsical collection of delightful books to make you think, chuckle, self-motivate & lift your spirits.

Road to Success

Motherhood

Kitty Litterature

Money

Computer Byte

View from Litter Box

ORDER ADDITIONAL BOOKS AS GIFTS

DOGGIE TALES   Qty_____ @ 7.95 Each _____

COMPUTER BYTE   Qty_____ @ 7.95 Each _____

MOTHERHOOD   Qty_____ @ 6.95 Each _____

VIEW FROM LITTER BOX Qty_____ @ 6.95 Each _____

KITTY LITTERATURE   Qty_____ @ 6.95 Each _____

THE ROAD TO SUCCESS   Qty_____ @ 6.95 Each _____

MONEY   Qty_____ @ 6.95 Each _____

GARDEN GROW   Qty_____ @ 6.95 Each _____

ACHIEVE YOUR DREAMS   Qty_____ @ 6.95 Each _____

Add 2.00 for shipping for 1st book, 50¢ ea. thereafter
WA State residents only: add applicable sales tax
Canadian & Foreign orders: double S & H charges & pay in US Funds
Order by phone: MasterCard / VISA accepted

Total _____

Send check with order

OR

```
Walrus Productions
4805 N.E. 106th St
Seattle, WA 98125
(206) 364-4365
```

Name _____

Address _____

City _____

State / Zip _____

Prices subject to change

These books may be ordered through your local book store.